Space to Stretch

Katelyn Pierce

BookLeaf
Publishing

India | USA | UK

Presentation by *BookLeaf Publishing*

Web: www.bookleafpub.com

E-mail: info@bookleafpub.com

ISBN: 978-93-5744-987-8

First edition 2022

DEDICATION

I'd like to dedicate this book to Alexandra and Alyssa. They let me text them a poem every day in our group chat and they never expressed an ounce of annoyance. I would have never found the motivation to finish this book without them.

Sweaty weather

Is it too much to ask for cardigans over
turtlenecks and skirts with opaque tights without
surfaces covered in water bottles and bare legs
covered in razor bumps and kitchen windows
that won't fully open even when you step on a
chair for leverage?

Half of us and a shaggy dog (needs a haircut!)
gather on a tight porch itching swollen bites
from little pests still alive. Next year, I'll wear
boots to Thanksgiving so they can't eat my
ankles.

More than a jellyfish

Girl's got that red vine spine

Wiggle it
trace the outline of your mouth
before you taste it and
suck it

She's got candy meant to
eat and
PLAY

You can even

sword fight and swing it!
helicopter and fling it!
Have all the fun you want cuz
red vines won't break
'til you bite

Candy the jawbreaker

Her name's Candy and
she's *special*.

Watch Candy thrust
her torso over a balcony
(thirty stories)
without dips in her belly or beads on
her lip.
Drape Candy's shoulders with
venomous snakes and
find wonderment in the
peak of her brows.
Show Candy her future —
stretchy neck skin without
pride for solace —
and see
nothing
but nonchalance.

Ask Candy if she's
SURE
she's okay —

feel Candy fondly brush
your arm and hear
Candy dramatically drawl *of cooooourse*!

Tell Candy you're unhappy and
watch Candy
caramelize.

Fandomination! (Kim Namjoon doesn't know we're married)

I'm in love with their design
curated perfectly by me and
everyone like me.
Hired for our desire, we record
their thoughts, style their dreams,
produce their Souls.
We are the faceless names and nameless faces
stitching childhood expectations
into intangible gods.
Possessed by my creation, I'm
my artists' artist.
But they'll never meet their maker!

Hold

We're born destined for hands
when we bend,
turn,
lie,
stand.
Symbiosis at its
finest —
hands wake the
flesh and flesh
wakes the man.

Hands reach in
things we wear.
Hands squeeze what's
covered or bare.
Whoever the body,
hands don't care.
Yelling or silent,
hands are there.

Tickle the horny
stress clown

I wake up with Tickle.

He sits between my tits
and makes me squirm and itch.

I push him aside to check my phone and
check my lists but it's *always*
time for Tickle!

He smiles when he grabs
the fat of my thighs
and

makes me laugh until I cry.

Boys n babes

Can you pinpoint the day you signed them
away?

Was it the time your cat chose to use them for
dough, or when that chill through your skin
really started to show?

Did your first purchase with mum put some pink
in your face, or was it that man lurking thrice
your young age?

It must have occurred when you bought your
shirts roomy

or maybe it was when you asked him to
"do me."

Whenever it happened, you know to your core
that what's on your chest wasn't meant to be
yours.

Well before infants can stake their true claims,
we give them away,
and we can't sign our names.

Walking the dogs

My septum scares 'em stiff!
It's not real, doesn't suit me, nose
drips, hurts to wipe
but everyone in the bushes knows
I'm a bull not a belle

I forget it's in and I flinch when I itch
cuz it likes to *pinch* but
nobody's coming
for septum girl.

…

Take it out.

Ankle biters useless as
tits, blanched ice knuckles on leash, heavy
bad knee and
quiet caught scream

Then –
phone snatched! mouth cupped! body dragged!
(oof)

But when both sides of my fake septum
magnetize together,
I got armour.

A big fat loser doing
big fat loser things

You dream to have eyes,
I've no clue of your reason.
Gotta
be noisier, flashier,
stinkier even.

Gotta
push on my back
to get through a crowd
Gotta
rev your dumb engine cuz
you live to be loud.
Gotta
drop subtle hints
of the money you make
Gotta
spit your big words —
it's *imitation*, not
fake!

If your cologne doesn't linger,
were you ever here?
Was it even a joke
if the room doesn't clear?
Try as you might,
you won't get my fear.
Please shut the hell up!
You're embarrassing, dear.

The most fun you'll ever have after a long and tiring work week!

Your throat splits and temples ache screaming over dreadful bass.

There's a careless jostle of your purse, but etiquette here's impaired as thoroughly as brains soaked in alcohol (no apology).

Niggling self-consciousness erupts inside while you get in her face and blow hot breath in her ear.

The smell of Caesar-in-an-empty-stomach can't appeal to her, but she said "what?" and forced your closeness.

Another jostle, equally careless.

You can dance, but not with them, not here. Your knees bend and straighten with the beat, and you know a lyric or three to mouth.

This time it's no jostle; it's a full-force shove. Maybe they're trying to rob you?

If they did, no one would see. To blend means to belong and you're more blended than vodka in soda here.

But *hey*!

At least you can tell your friends you got robbed and they'd (probably?) let you leave.

Netflix decorum

Unblinking, we're fixed to
faces of rehearsed pain.
Downloadable.

They
leak through the screen
crash, grip, permeate our chests
Trickle

in

so

slowly

and then all at once!

Waves build and curl inside
climbing higher, filling our throats
swollen deep and
aching, spilling without permission and
washing up cheap sympathy.

Peripherals show
frantic wiping in low light,
but we hide our wet sleeves or collars
and slimy noses.

A room of puffy faces under a surface no one
dares break.
No one dares turn, no one dares acknowledge.
I'm exposed in open waters with
three vegan sharks,
shivery but safe.

Fragile friendship

I promise
when I tell her I'll be

careful,
like a Bell employee installing a screen protector
(two bubbles and a tiny hair)

gentle,
like a shelter volunteer bathing feral cats
(oodles of blood and skin surrendered)

thoughtful,
like an overworked mom explaining mortality
(life sucks then you die, sweetie)

tenderly, lovingly,

I'll tell her about that booger.

Life lesson

Good morning class!
Today we're going to talk about the less
fortunate.

She goes to bed partnerless,
limbs space to starfish, damp breath off her neck
She wakes up childless,
nothing to feed or bathe or soothe.

Eyes at the front!
joy + love = mom + wife
I don't see all of you writing this down.

You!
joyless, loveless girl by the window!
no one gave you permission to be content!

The proposal

She said,
"If you love me let me go"
He said,
"I do love you so you'll stay"

Settled, she settled
and settled

Love in the time of Tinder

Focus floats
before you push it from a plane.
Down,
down.
Sometimes fast and furious,
often, slow and secretive (with a parachute).
His temple pimple's roaring to pop
and his lips need a little lick.

Adjacent man politely laughs rogue lash breaks
into eye poem starts to write calamari takes
too long parachute won't open stomach
whines for calamari fluffy gnocchi
begs for bite prospective
cheesecake
elbows
through

cheesecake
CHEESECAKE
Cheeeeesecaaaaake!

…

You're half dead.
He's floated away.
But there's still dessert!

One more word and I'm getting my boots on!

I gave you everything I know.

1. My view
2. My past
3. My colours

Yet
you didn't know I'd kick you in the shin
for that stupid fucking comment?

Call me captain

Set sail for this ceaseless process,
pay again for weakness,
watch the ad roll in, the CVV roll out, and
see there's no confirmation for sickness.
Find treasure chests full of weight
open to bring shimmer to empty eyes and
close to
repackage the darkness.

Plead for deliverance to pay and
pay again.

At least this ship sinks for free.

Bday night raw

The match is fixed but I always tune in.

"In this corner,
our reigning champ,
LITTLE BABY K!"
(K growls under sunflower bucket hat
and twirls jump rope like a lasso)

"And in this corner,
a brand new challenger,
CRUSTY MISS P!"
(Hag with wilting boobies
and hay hair swallows acid reflux)

"Crusty P dragged her chronically fatigued
and stretch-marked ass out
a skid marked toilet bowl
splattered with financial insecurity
and shopping addiction
to give our Little K
the BEAT-DOWN of her
peach-fuzz-legs-having-
LIFE!"

Crowd boos and hurls
rusty car parts at P,
leaky battery whacks P
in the back of her dry scalp

Pulse check for P!

Crowd chants *rip*, *rip*, *rip* while P's
machine cog corpse is carried
out.

Pause.

…

"FOR THE 28TH YEAR IN A ROW!
YOUR CHAMPION!
LITTLE! BABY! K!"

Build-a-Bear clothes, Halloween candy,
and RESP contributions
flood the ring

Pushing thirty

Time swells with the
crease by your mouth
and the ache through your back
and the fatigue
in your spirit

No consent, no goal posts,
just people you know
going around
[un]fulfilling potentials

Your sister and her friend's sister swell
next to the expiring prospects of
the people they know.
One day, they'll swell to burst
new potential, new time into life

all while you and the others grow
tired.

2020-?

If
they don't like needles and
they won't wear masks
they can't take an empathy pill
strong enough to save them

My moth

There was a moth in my bedroom. It wouldn't stay still. It kept flittering and fluttering from my ceiling to my walls and was uncharacteristically disinterested in my lamp. Its quick movements unsettled me when I settled under my covers.

I tried to keep an eye on it but I'm near-sighted and I take my glasses off for bed. I put the bathroom light on, tried to lure it away, but it determinedly stayed. I took my bucket hat, stood on my bed, and smacked at the ceiling, but I got a tiny piece of the outdated popcorn in my eye (trickier and more painful to remove than anticipated).

It stayed for a couple more days, always making its frantic presence known when I wanted to rest.

Today, I spotted my moth while I was vacuuming my carpet. She finally stopped to take her own rest. I sucked her up as my eyes fluttered and burned.